W9-AVJ-846

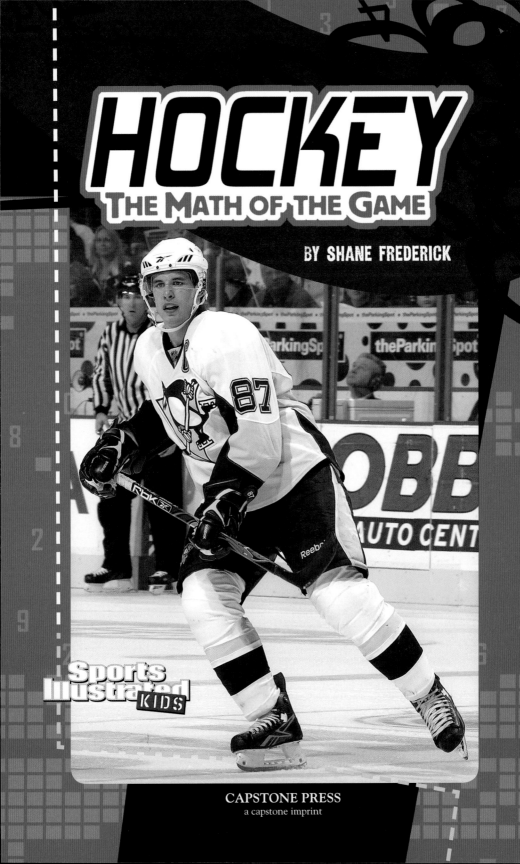

HOCKEY
THE MATH OF THE GAME

BY SHANE FREDERICK

CAPSTONE PRESS
a capstone imprint

Sports Illustrated KIDS Sports Math is published by Capstone Press,
1710 Roe Crest Drive, North Mankato, Minnesota 56003.
www.capstonepub.com

Books published by Capstone Press are manufactured with paper
containing at least 10 percent post-consumer waste.

Library of Congress Cataloging-in-Publication Data
Frederick, Shane.
  Hockey : the math of the game / by Shane Frederick.
    p. cm.—(Sports illustrated KIDS. Sports math)
  Includes bibliographical references and index.
  Summary: "Presents the mathematical concepts involved with the sport of hockey"—
Provided by publisher.
  ISBN 978-1-4296-6570-4 (library binding)
  ISBN 978-1-4296-7321-1 (paperback)
  1. Hockey—Mathematics—Juvenile literature. I. Title. II. Series.
  GV847.25.F735 2012
  796.962—dc22   2011007865

Editorial Credits
Anthony Wacholtz, editor; Alison Thiele, designer; Eric Gohl, media researcher;
    Eric Manske, production specialist

Photo Credits
Dreamstime/Gale Verhague, cover (back), 6–7
Newscom/Icon SMI 114/Jeanine Leech, 41
Shutterstock/Debra Hughes, design element; Petr Vaclavek, design element;
    Rocket400 Studio, 15, 25 (bottom), 43
Sports Illustrated/Bob Rosato, 23 (bottom); Damian Strohmeyer, 13
    (bottom), 27 (bottom); David E. Klutho, cover (front), 1, 4–5, 8, 9, 10, 11, 12–13,
    16, 17, 18, 19, 21, 22, 23 (top), 26, 27 (top), 28, 30, 31, 33, 34–35, 36, 37, 38, 39, 40,
    42, 44; Robert Beck, 14, 20, 24, 25, 29, 32, 35 (bottom); Walter Iooss Jr., 45

Printed in the United States of America in Stevens Point, Wisconsin.
052012   006770R

TABLE OF CONTENTS

⬚ ORDER IN THE CHAOS

Hockey is one of the fastest, roughest games out there. Players practically fly around the arena, gliding on their skates. They collide in the middle of the ice, and they smash each other into the boards around the rink. All the while, the players chase a small, black puck zigzagging around their feet while trying to shoot it into the other team's goal.

With all of that chaos going on, would you believe that the players are also doing math? It's true. During a game players are counting numbers, contemplating ratios, and studying angles. They're measuring space, keeping time, and calculating statistics. And they're doing it all with skates on their feet and a stick in their hands. Math not only helps them understand the game of hockey, but it helps them play it too.

Math can also help fans better appreciate and enjoy the game. So grab your favorite jersey and a calculator, and get ready for some hockey!

THE BASICS

CHAPTER 1

INSIDE THE BOARDS

Hockey is played on an ice rink, which is a sheet of ice surrounded by walls made of boards and glass. A National Hockey League (NHL) rink is 200 feet long and 85 feet wide. It's big enough to have room for 12 players (five skaters and a goalie on each team), as well as four game officials.

The rink isn't an exact rectangle. It has rounded corners. But to get an estimate of the skating area, multiply the rink's length by its width.

area = 200 feet * 85 feet = 17,000 square feet

A square foot is a space that is one foot long and one foot wide. We can also figure out the area of the team's attacking/defensive zone and the area of the neutral zone.

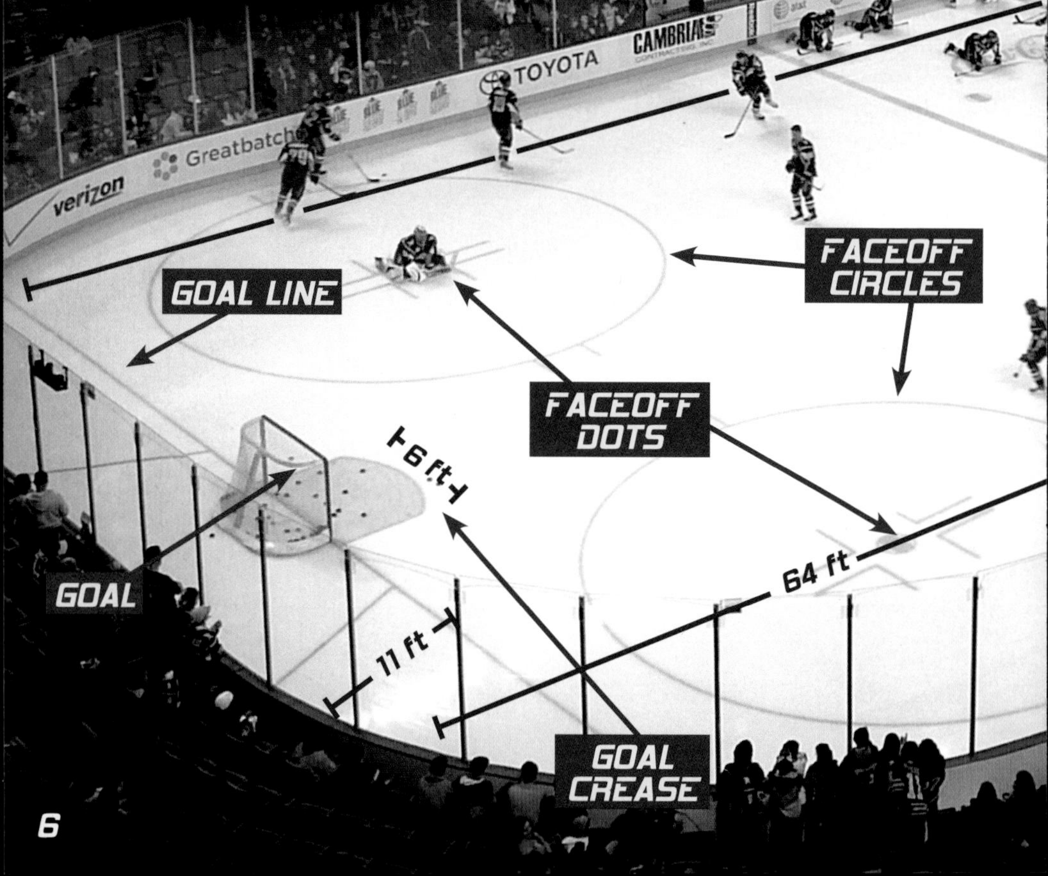

StateFarm
CAMBRIA
TOYOTA
Greatbatch
verizon
FACEOFF CIRCLES
GOAL LINE
FACEOFF DOTS
6 ft
GOAL
64 ft
11 ft
GOAL CREASE

Attacking/Defensive Zone: **75 feet * 85 feet = 6.375 square feet**

Neutral Zone: **50 feet * 85 feet = 4.250 square feet**

Olympic-sized rinks are used in international play, as well as by European pro teams and some American college teams. The rink is still 200 feet long, but it is 100 feet wide. The extra 15 feet of width might not seem like a lot. But if you do the math, there is an extra 3,000 square feet (200 feet * 15 feet) on the ice.

200 ft

85 ft

RED LINE

NEUTRAL ZONE

50 ft

BLUE LINES

THE GOAL

A player scores in hockey by shooting the puck past the goaltender and into the goal. A hockey goal is 6 feet wide and 4 feet high. With no goalie in the way, players have 24 square feet to aim for (6 feet * 4 feet).

ICE ALL AROUND

Most rinks have about 1 inch of ice. To measure the space that will be filled with frozen water, you must figure out the volume. Multiply the rink's length, width, and height.

200 feet * 85 feet * 1 inch

Don't forget to convert inches to feet. Since there are 12 inches in a foot, change 1 inch to $\frac{1}{12}$ of a foot (.0833).

200 feet * 85 feet * $\frac{1}{12}$ foot = about 1,417 cubic feet

There are about 7.5 gallons of water in one cubic foot. About how many gallons of water are needed to create a one-inch layer of ice in a standard hockey rink?

ANSWER: 10,628 gallons

After 20 minutes of the players' skates cutting through the ice, the playing surface is no longer smooth. The bumps and ridges cause the puck to bounce, and the players have a harder time skating.

To keep the ice smooth, a resurfacing machine, such as a Zamboni, comes onto the ice after each period. The machine adds warm water to the ice that will fill in the gaps as it freezes. The machine also cleans the surface of any dirt and debris. The result is a smooth ice surface that is as good as new.

ZAMBONI

In the NHL two resurfacing machines smooth the ice at one time. Each machine travels about 0.75 miles during one resurfacing. The ice is usually resurfaced before the game, after warm-ups, between periods, and after the game.

The machines can only travel up to nine miles per hour. If the machine traveled at its top speed for each resurfacing, how long would it take to do all five resurfaces?

First we need to find out how much distance the resurfacing machine travels for all five resurfaces.

$$0.75 \text{ miles} * 5 \text{ resurfaces} = 3.75 \text{ miles}$$

Then divide the number of miles covered by the speed of the resurfacing machine.

$$\frac{3.75 \text{ miles}}{9 \text{ miles/hour}} = 0.42 \text{ hours}$$

It would take the resurfacing machines a little less than half an hour to do all five resurfaces. That's quick work!

SHIFT WORK

Professional hockey games are 60 minutes long, with three 20-minute periods. But did you know that most skaters play only for about 15 minutes per game? That's less than one period!

Teams play in shifts, with groups of three forwards (called lines) and pairs of defensemen regularly changing on the fly. Each shift lasts roughly 45 seconds, and players go all out during that time, making the most of their shift.

To figure out a player's time on the ice for a game, add up the time of each shift. You'll find that defensemen usually play more minutes than forwards. The best players usually get the most ice time because they're on the ice for all situations—even strength, power plays, or penalty kills.

In 2009–2010 the Chicago Blackhawks' star defenseman, Duncan Keith, logged an average of 26 minutes, 35 seconds per game. The top forwards in the NHL for playing time were Ilya Kovalchuk, Sidney Crosby, Martin St. Louis, and Alex Ovechkin. Each of them averaged around 22 minutes per game.

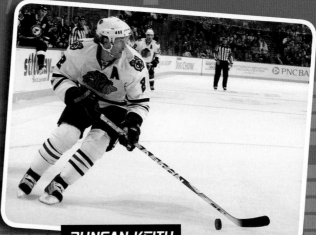

DUNCAN KEITH

In Game 6 of the 2010 Stanley Cup Finals, Keith got more ice time than anybody, playing 30 minutes, 39 seconds. With overtime the game lasted 64 minutes, 6 seconds.

What percentage of the game did Keith play? First figure out how many seconds he played.

playing time =
(30 minutes * 60 seconds/minute) + 39 seconds

playing time =
1,800 seconds + 39 seconds = 1,839 seconds

Then calculate how many seconds there were in the entire game.

game time =
(64 minutes * 60 seconds/minute) + 6 seconds

game time =
3,840 seconds + 6 seconds = 3,846 seconds

Finally divide Keith's playing time by the total game time.

1,839 seconds / 3,846 seconds = 47.8 percent

Keith spent almost half the game on the ice!

If the average shift is 45 seconds, about how many shifts did Keith play?

ANSWER: 41 shifts

Geometry can be found all over the ice rink. For the team with the puck, the ability to understand and use angles is almost like having an extra player on the ice. Players use the boards surrounding the ice as the extra players. Rather than try to skate or make a pass through a defender who might steal the puck, players often chip the puck against the boards. That way the puck deflects to a teammate on the other side of the defending player.

When an object deflects off a flat surface, it bounces off at an angle equal to the one it came in on. In physics this is called the angle of incidence (the puck being passed toward the boards) being equal to the angle of reflection (the puck bouncing off the boards).

Think of one arm of an angle being the path of the puck and the other as an imaginary line running perpendicular from the boards. Where the puck hits the boards is the vertex. So if the puck is chipped to the boards at a 45-degree angle, it will reflect at a 45-degree angle. If the puck is chipped at a 15-degree angle, it will come off the boards at a 15-degree angle.

45°

45°

The player making the pass has to understand the angles to get the puck to a teammate. The pass receiver must also understand angles in order to make sure he or she skates to where the puck will end up.

BEND THOSE KNEES!

From the time they first learn to skate, hockey players are told to bend their knees. A good knee bend can boost the power in a skater's stride. But it can also help a player cover more ice with his body and his stick. A player just has to understand triangles.

Think of a hockey player as one side of a right triangle. The hockey stick forms another side, and the ice between the player's skates and the end of his stick forms the other.

The Pythagorean theorem is a way to measure right triangles. The formula is $a^2 + b^2 = c^2$, with the letters representing each side. The letter **c** represents the hypotenuse, which is the side opposite the right angle.

ANZE KOPITAR

Anze Kopitar of the Los Angeles Kings is 6 feet 3 inches tall on skates. He probably has a 5-foot-long stick, which he holds near his chest, about 4 feet 4 inches high. How far in front can his stick reach while standing straight up? Use the Pythagorean theorem to measure. The player's height to the top of the stick is **a**, and the stick is **c**, so we must solve for **b**.

First convert feet to inches.

4 feet 4 inches = 52 inches

5 feet = 60 inches

Then plug in the numbers.

$$52^2 + b^2 = 60^2$$
$$2,704 + b^2 = 3,600$$
$$b^2 = 3,600 - 2,704$$
$$b^2 = 896$$

Then take the square root of both sides to solve for **b**.

b = 29.9 inches

So standing straight up, Kopitar can reach about 30 inches, or 2½ feet, in front of him with his stick.

But what if he bends his knees? How much ice can he cover if his knees are bent 6 inches? What about a foot?

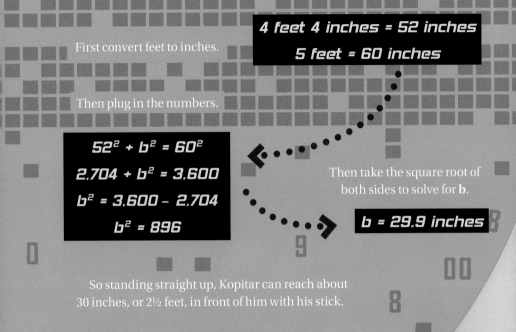

6 inches:
$$46^2 + b^2 = 60^2$$
$$2116 + b^2 = 3,600$$
$$b^2 = 1,484$$
$$\sqrt{1,484} = 38.5$$

12 inches:
$$40^2 + b^2 = 60^2$$
$$1600 + b^2 = 3,600$$
$$b^2 = 2,000$$
$$\sqrt{2,000} = 44.7$$

With his knees bent so that the stick is one foot lower, Kopitar can cover the ice 44.7 inches, or almost 4 feet, in front of him!

CHAPTER 2

Goals are not easy to come by in hockey. Scoring is hard work for teams and players. In 2010–2011 the Detroit Red Wings were one of the highest-scoring teams in the NHL. But the team only averaged a little more than three goals per game. That season the Red Wings scored a total of 257 goals over the 82-game season.

To determine the average of goals scored per game, divide the number of goals by the number of games.

257 goals / 82 games = 3.13 goals/game

In 1920 the Montreal Canadiens scored
16 goals in a win over the Quebec Bulldogs.
It's an NHL record that still stands.

In 2010–2011 the Vancouver Canucks fired 2,757 shots on opposing goaltenders. That means a fairly low percentage of shots got past the goalie and into the net. To figure out the percentage of shots scored, divide the goals scored by the number of shots taken.

257 goals / 2,757 shots on goal = 0.093

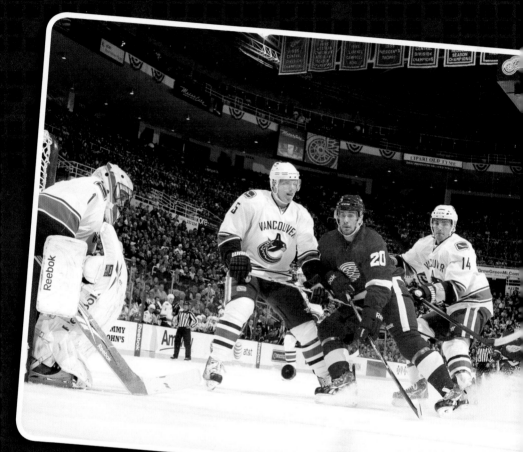

Then multiply the result by 100 to get the percentage. The Canucks made 9.3 percent of their shots.

The highest-scoring team in NHL history was the 1983–1984 Edmonton Oilers. Led by superstar Wayne Gretzky, the Oilers scored 446 goals in 80 games. The team also put 2,613 shots on goal that season. What was their average goals per game? What was their shot percentage?

ANSWER: 5.575 goals/game; 17% shot percentage

GOALS + ASSISTS = POINTS

When goals finally do go in, hockey doesn't let the players who finish the play get all of the glory. The sport also rewards the playmakers, giving points to players who make the passes that lead up to the goal.

When a goal is scored in a game, official scorers can award zero, one, or two assists. Add a player's goals and assists to get the point total. The NHL's scoring champion each year is not the player who has the most goals but the most points.

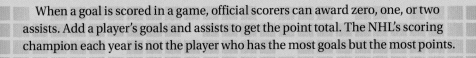

Hockey's greatest all-time player, Wayne Gretzky, finished his NHL career with 894 goals and 1,963 assists. Nobody scored more goals or assists. Add those together and you get 2,857 points.

Gretzky owns the NHL's four best scoring seasons. Fill in the missing numbers from those seasons:

YEAR	GOALS	ASSISTS	POINTS
1985–1986	52	A	215
1981–1982	92	120	B
1984–1985	C	135	208
1983–1984	87	118	D

ANSWER: A: 163; B: 212; C: 73; D: 205

How dominant was Gretzky? Take away his goals, and he still has more points than the league's second-best point scorer, Mark Messier. Messier finished his career with 1,887 points. He scored 694 goals and had 1,193 assists. The great Gordie Howe comes in at a close third place with 1,850 points. He had 801 goals and 1,049 assists.

WAYNE GRETZKY

When a player scores three goals in a single game, it is called a hat trick.

POWER PLAYS

During a hockey game, each team has five skaters and a goalie on the ice—most of the time. But when a player commits a penalty, he or she must get off the ice. The player has to stay in the penalty box for at least two minutes, or until the other team scores a goal. That player cannot be replaced, meaning the penalized team must play with one fewer player.

It gives the other team an advantage because it's more difficult for four defenders to cover five players. It's even tougher if two players get penalties and the team only has three players and the goalie on the ice. Teams cannot play with fewer than three skaters on the ice.

When a team plays with one or two more players on the ice than the other team, it is called a power play. The team with fewer players is playing short-handed for the penalty kill.

The best teams in the NHL score goals on power plays 25 percent of the time. To figure out a team's power play percentage:

$$\frac{\text{power play goals}}{\text{power play opportunities}} = \text{power play \%}$$

In 2010–2011 Vancouver was the top power play team in the NHL, scoring 62 goals on 256 chances. The Canucks' power play percentage was 24.3% (72 / 296).

The best penalty kill teams stop around 85 percent of opponents' scoring during power plays. That means they allow one goal in every six or seven kills. Use division to figure out a team's penalty kill success rate.

$$\frac{successful\ kills}{total\ penalty\ kills} = penalty\ kill\ \%$$

In 2010–2011 the Pittsburgh Penguins were one of the best penalty-killing teams in the NHL, allowing 45 goals on 325 penalty kills. What was their success rate?

PITTSBURGH PENGUINS

First figure out the number of successful kills.

325 penalty kills – 45 goals = 280 successful penalty kills

Then divide by the number of total penalty kills.

$$\frac{280\ successful\ penalty\ kills}{325\ total\ penalty\ kills} = 86.2\ penalty\ kill\ \%$$

Math symbols are used to figure out equations, but they can also be seen in a hockey rink every night. Statisticians not only keep track of goals, assists, shots on goal, and saves, but also plus-minus (+/-).

Plus-minus marks the number of goals scored for a player's team and the opponent while a certain player was on the ice. It's a good way to gauge players who are more defensive-minded. Power-play goals do not count for or against a player's plus-minus statistic, but a short-handed goal does.

ZDENO CHARA

Zdeno Chara of the Boston Bruins was the 2010–2011 NHL leader in plus-minus with a +33. If Chara is on the ice for three of his team's goals and one of the opponent's goals, he would have a +2 for the game.

In another game let's say Chara is on the ice for one of his team's power-play goals, two of the opponent's even-strength goals, and one of his opponent's power-play goals. The power play goals don't count against plus-minus, so Chara has a -2 for the game.

Imagine if Patrik Elias of the New Jersey Devils scores a hat trick, but he wasn't playing during any of his team's other goals. He was also on the ice for a goal by the Philadelphia Flyers. What was his plus-minus?

ANSWER: +2

PATRIK ELIAS

Steven Stamkos of the Tampa Bay Lightning scores a short-handed goal, and the Dallas Stars score a power-play goal while he's on the ice. What is his plus-minus?

ANSWER: +1

STEVEN STAMKOS

The best plus-minus rating for a single season was in 1970–1971. Boston Bruins defenseman Bobby Orr was a +124.

SLAP SHOT GEOMETRY

One of the most exciting plays in hockey is the slap shot. That's when a player has enough time and space to fire a powerful shot that rockets toward the goal as fast as 100 miles per hour. Over time slap shots have become harder, thanks to lighter sticks and bigger, stronger players.

Modern sticks are made of composite materials such as carbon fiber, graphite, and fiberglass. The materials allow sticks to flex during a shot.

The bend of the stick harnesses the shooter's energy as the blade of the stick hits the ice just before it hits the puck. When the stick snaps back into shape during the follow-through, the energy is released, sending the puck whizzing toward the goalie.

A hockey stick can flex up to a 30-degree angle. Too much flex will cause the stick to break. To see what the angle looks like, think of the shooter's lower hand as the vertex, the stick as one arm and the invisible straight line from the hand to the ice as the other arm.

30°

Without the flex, a hockey stick is still at an angle. It is 180 degrees, also known as a straight angle. Two angles that add up to 180 degrees are called supplementary angles.

If a player gets a 30-degree flex on a shot, what is the supplementary angle? What is the supplementary angle for a 22-degree flex?

ANSWER: 150 degrees, 158 degrees

CHAPTER 3

DEFENSE — WHAT A GOALIE!

The best goaltenders give up the fewest number of goals to help their teams win games. There are two major statistics that are used to compare goaltenders: goals-against average (GAA) and save percentage (SV%).

GAA measures the number of goals per game a goaltender allows over the season. To measure GAA take the total number of goals a goalie allows and divide that by the number of games played. First take the total number of minutes played. Then add overtime minutes and subtract time out of the net. Divide the result by the number of minutes in a regulation game (60 minutes in the NHL).

total minutes / 60 = games played

GAA = goals allowed / games played

The Bruins' Tim Thomas had the lowest goals-against average in the NHL in 2010–2011. That season he played 3,364 minutes and allowed 112 goals. What was his GAA?

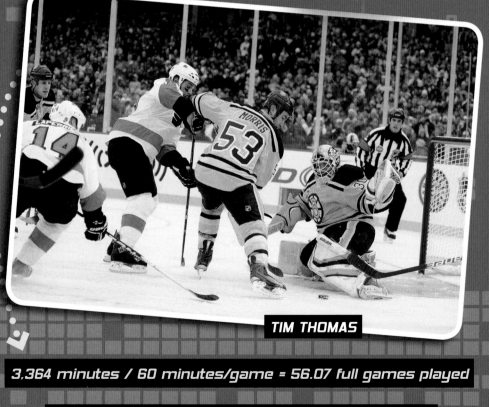

TIM THOMAS

3,364 minutes / 60 minutes/game = 56.07 full games played

112 goals allowed / 56.07 games played = 2.00 GAA

Save percentage measures how often a goalie stops a shot on goal. The best goalies usually have a save percentage of .910 (91 percent). To get the save percentage, divide the number of saves by the total number of shots on goal (saves plus goals).

saves / shots on goal = SV%

JOSE THEODORE

In 2001–2002 the Montreal Canadiens' Jose Theodore led the league in save percentage. He faced 1,972 shots and allowed 136 goals. That means he had 1,836 saves (1,972 – 136) for a .931 save percentage.

Which goalie had the best save percentage during the 2010–2011 season?

PLAYER	SHOTS ON GOAL	SAVES
MARC-ANDRE FLEURY	1,742	1,599
CAM WARD	2,375	2,191
ILYA BRYZGALOV	2,125	1,957

ANSWER: Cam Ward
(Ward: .923; Bryzgalov: .921; Fleury: .918)

CAM WARD

One big thing stands in the way of a shooter and a goal—the goaltender. The goalie's job is to stop the puck from going in the net. There are many ways goalies can block the puck. They can catch it with their oversized gloves, turn it away with their stick, kick it with their big shin pads or skates, or simply get in the puck's way.

Even with all of their gear, goalies only take up about 60 percent of the goal area. That means 40 percent of the goal is still open. Shooters try to hit those open spots with their shots. They practice putting the puck into those small spaces, often aiming as close to the metal pipes surrounding the goal as possible. Also, by stickhandling and passing the puck, shooters try to get the goalie to move around in order to open up bigger spaces to hit.

An NHL rule states that a goalie's leg pads cannot be more than 11 inches wide. So if the goalie lays down to block a shot, the pair of stacked pads covers 22 inches in height. That works for low shots, but how much of the goal is left open? A goal is 48 inches high, so 26 inches (54 percent) of the net is exposed.

Goaltenders have another weapon besides size, quickness, and equipment to use against shooters. Goalies can use angles to keep themselves between the puck and the goal.

Imagine the puck as the vertex of an angle, with the two angle arms (rays) drawn out to each goal post. The goaltender's job is to stay centered within that angle to take up as much of the goal as possible.

Goalies can cut down the angle by moving out of the goal toward the shooter and shortening the space they see between angle arms. They can't move out too far, however, because it will leave the goal wide open for another attacking player or a deflected puck.

Goal scorers understand angles too. For shooters, the bigger the angle, the better chance they have to score.

Angles are measured in degrees. A shot from a 45-degree angle from inside the faceoff dots has a better chance of hitting the net than a shot from a 10-degree angle from along the goal line.

QUICK REACTION

No matter what area of the net goalies concentrate on, they still leave part of the net open. A puck could easily deflect off a stick or skates. In order to stop those shots, goalies must also have a quick reaction time. How quick? Well, for a shot coming at them from beyond the blue line at 90 miles per hour—a shot most goalies are expected to stop—they have less than half a second to make the save. As attacking players move the puck closer to the net, goalies have even less time to react to a shot.

SPEEDY SHOT

The hardest shots in the NHL fly at a blistering 100 miles per hour or more. Boston Bruins defenseman Zdeno Chara fired a slap shot 105.9 mph during a skills competition at the All-Star Game in 2011.

To calculate how much time it takes for a goalie to make a save, you can use this equation.

time = distance / rate

First turn the miles per hour into feet per second. There are 5,280 feet in a mile and 3,600 seconds in an hour. In the case of a 90 mile-per-hour shot, multiply 90 by the number of feet in a mile. Then divide by the number of seconds in an hour.

90 mph * 5,280 feet/mile = 475,200 feet/hour

475,200 feet/hour / 3,600 seconds/hour = 132 feet/second

With a puck shot at 90 miles per hour from about 60 feet away, how much time does the goalie have to make the save?

60 feet / 132 feet/second = .454 seconds

PEKKA RINNE

Can you figure out how much time Pekka Rinne of the Nashville Predators would have to stop an 80 mile-per-hour slap shot from the faceoff circle 20 feet away?

ANSWER:
0.170 seconds

THE RED ZONE

Now that you know about reaction time and angles, you can probably guess from where most of the goals are scored. There is an area that some coaches call the red zone that covers the space between the goal and the faceoff dots inside the offensive zone. The area forms the shape of a trapezoid.

A high percentage of goals are scored in that area. Outside of that area, a player's chances of scoring go down. Why? On the sides of the goal, the angles are smaller, which make the shots more difficult. Also, shots fired from farther out give goalies more reaction time to see the puck and make a save.

Defending players often try to steer attacking players outside of the trapezoid, pushing the puck carriers out toward the boards and the blue line or down below the goal line. They also try to keep the puck out of the middle of the rink. They work the angles by keeping themselves between the puck and the goal while blocking shooting and passing lanes. Goaltenders also try to control the puck by deflecting rebounds to the side, rather than to the dangerous middle of the rink.

PATRICK KANE

Patrick Kane's game-winning goal in overtime of the 2010 Stanley Cup finals came from a very small angle outside the scoring zone. For a few moments, the fans didn't realize the Chicago Blackhawks had just won the Stanley Cup.

APPLYING THE MATH

PREDICTIONS

Derek Stepan of the New York Rangers started his 2010–2011 season by scoring a hat trick. What kind of a season can you expect from him? If you do the math and multiply three goals times the regular-season's 82 games, Stepan was on pace for a 246-goal season. Talk about the next Great One!

DEREK
STEPAN

But is that realistic? Not when the all-time single-season record for goals is 92 set by the real Great One, Wayne Gretzky, in 1981–1982. Gretzky played in 80 games that season and averaged 1.15 goals per game.

A simple formula called cross multiplication can be used to make a guess of a player's stats from a small sample. We can predict Stepan's season goal total from his first 10 games using cross multiplication. Stepan scored three goals in 10 games, but we want to know how many he will score in 82 games.

$$\frac{3}{10} = \frac{x}{82}$$

Cross multiply and solve for x, the number of goals we are predicting Stepan will score.

$$3 * 82 = 10 * x$$

$$246 = 10x$$

Then divide both sides by 10 to leave x by itself.

$$\frac{246}{10} = \frac{10x}{10}$$

$$x = 246 / 10$$

$$x = 24.6$$

From only 10 games of stats, we can predict that Stepan will end the season with about 25 goals. In reality, Stepan scored 21 goals—pretty close!

In 2010–2011 the Canucks' Daniel Sedin won the NHL scoring title with 104 points in 82 games. Use cross multiplication to see what pace Sedin was on through one game, 10 games, 20 games, and the season's halfway point.

DANIEL SEDIN

1 GAME	1 POINT
10 GAMES	12 POINTS
20 GAMES	24 POINTS
41 GAMES	54 POINTS

ANSWER: one game = 82 points; 10 games = 98.4 points; 20 games = 98.4 points; 41 games = 108 points

In the NHL the ultimate goal is to win the Stanley Cup. But in order to do that, a team must first make the playoffs following a grinding 82-game regular season schedule. There are 30 teams in the NHL, and 16 of them advance to the postseason. What percentage of the teams make it to the playoffs? Divide the number of playoff teams by the total number of teams.

$$16 / 30 = .533$$

That means 53.3 percent of the league—a little more than half—advances to the playoffs.

The NHL is divided into two conferences—the Eastern Conference and the Western Conference. Each conference has three divisions, each with five teams. At the end of the season, each of the six division champions makes the playoffs. The next five best teams from each conference fill out the remaining spots.

The top team in the NHL standings is usually the team with the most wins. Hockey uses a point system for its standings, awarding a team two points for a win and one point for a team that loses in overtime or in a penalty-shot shootout. The shootout started in the 2005–2006 season. Before then regular-season games could end in a tie.

Once the playoff field is set, what chance does a team have of winning it all? Since there are 16 teams in the playoffs, they have a 1 in 16 chance (6.25 percent). As teams are eliminated, the remaining teams' chances of winning go up.

A team's chance of winning goes up after each round:	
16 TEAMS	6.25 %
8 TEAMS	12.5 %
4 TEMS	25%
2 TEAMS	50%

Detroit Red Wings fans have a slimy playoff tradition. During a home game, someone will throw a dead octopus onto the ice. This dates back to when there were just six teams in the NHL and the top four made it to the postseason. Each of the octopus' legs represented one of eight wins it took to win the prized Stanley Cup.

Today NHL teams have to win more than eight games. Each round of the playoffs is a best-of-seven matchup. That means a team has to win four games in the series to advance. To take home the Stanley Cup, a team has to win four series.

How many games does a team need to win to become champions?

ANSWER: 16

SHARING THE GOALS

The Chicago Blackhawks scored 29 goals over six games on the way to capturing the 2010 Stanley Cup. Fourteen players scored goals, including Patrick Kane, who clinched the series victory with a game-winning goal in overtime of Game 6. To get a look at how the goals were distributed, you can use a pie chart to see how big of a chunk each scorer contributed to the win.

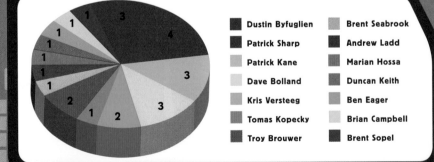

BLACKHAWKS' GOALS: 2010 FINALS

- Dustin Byfuglien
- Patrick Sharp
- Patrick Kane
- Dave Bolland
- Kris Versteeg
- Tomas Kopecky
- Troy Brouwer
- Brent Seabrook
- Andrew Ladd
- Marian Hossa
- Duncan Keith
- Ben Eager
- Brian Campbell
- Brent Sopel

Patrick Sharp scored the most goals, finding the back of the net four times. That is about 13.8 percent of the team's 29 goals. Kane, Dave Bolland, and Dustin Byfuglien each had three goals, getting a slightly smaller chunk of the pie (10.3 percent).

The Blackhawks' opponent was the Philadelphia Flyers. The Flyers had 12 players score 22 goals in the series. Take a look at their pie chart and answer the two questions below about their goal distribution.

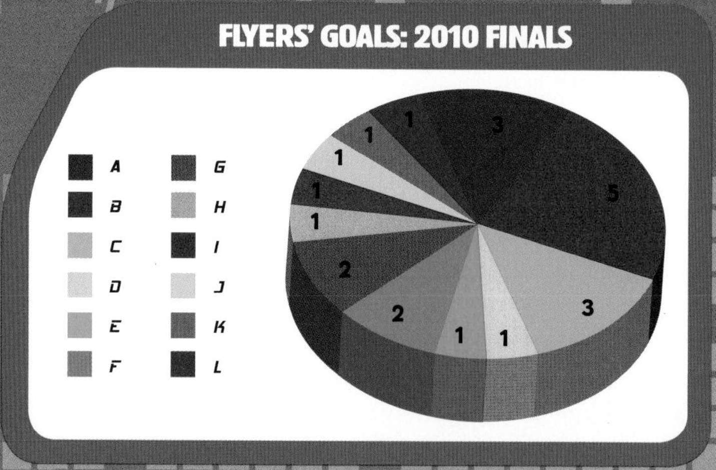

FLYERS' GOALS: 2010 FINALS

A
B
C
D
E
F
G
H
I
J
K
L

Scott Hartnell scored the most goals for the Flyers with five. Which piece of the pie does he represent? What percent of the team's goals did he score?

ANSWER: B; 22.7%

How many Flyers players scored one goal during the Stanley Cup Finals? If you add their goals together, what percent of the team's goals did they score?

ANSWER: seven players; 31.8%

39

Looking at a player's averages is a good way to measure his or her value. But there are other ways of breaking down those numbers over time. Figuring out the mean (average), median, mode, and range from a list of numbers can tell us a lot about a player's stats.

One of the best players in the NHL today is the Calgary Flames' Jarome Iginla. Let's take a look at his year-by-year point totals and break down his career stats. (Note: There was no 2004–2005 season because of a dispute between players and owners.)

Season	Points
1996–1997	50
1997–1998	32
1998–1999	51
1999–2000	63
2000–2001	71
2001–2002	96
2002–2003	67
2003–2004	73
2005–2006	67
2006–2007	94
2007–2008	98
2008–2009	89
2009–2010	69
2010–2011	86
TOTAL	1,006

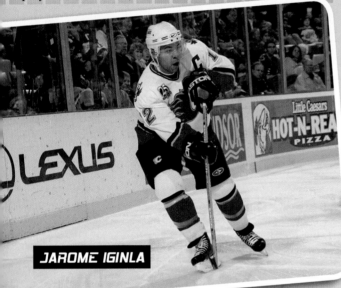

JAROME IGINLA

What are Iginla's mean points over his career so far? In other words, how many points did Iginla average per season? Simply divide the total points by the number of seasons he played.

$$1,006 / 14 = 71.9$$

Iginla has averaged 71.9 points per season through the 2010–2011 season. Next let's look at his median, mode, and range.

mean—the average amount of a set of numbers

median—the middle number in a list of numbers

mode—the number in a list that is repeated most often

range—the difference between the largest and smallest value

To get the median, mode, and range, organize the numbers from lowest to highest.

32 50 51 63 67 67 69 71 73 86 89 94 96 98

Because there is an even number of entries in the list, the median is actually two numbers: 69 and 71. The mode is 67—it's the only number that appears twice. To find the range, subtract the lowest value from the highest value: 98 – 32 = 66.

Notice that his numbers are all very similar. That means he's had a consistent career. Who wouldn't want Jarome Iginla on his or her fantasy team?

Let's look at the point totals for another star player, the Tampa Bay Lightning's Vincent Lecavalier.

1998–1999	28
1999–2000	67
2000–2001	51
2001–2002	37
2002–2003	78
2003–2004	66
2005–2006	75
2006–2007	108
2007–2008	92
2008–2009	67
2009–2010	70
2010–2011	54
TOTAL	793

VINCENT LECAVALIER

Can you determine Lecavalier's mean, median, mode, and range?

ANSWER: mean: 66.1; median: 67; mode: 67; range: 80

PLOTTING THE STATS

During the 2010–2011 season, the Vancouver Canucks won the President's Trophy as the NHL team that accumulated the most points from wins and overtime losses. The Canucks went 54–19–9 for 117 points, winning the Northwest Division. They also led the NHL in goal scoring with 258 goals.

Does goal scoring equal wins? One way to find out if that is a trend is by using a scatter plot, which is a graph that allows you to track correlating statistics. In this case you can pinpoint where a team's goals match its team points on a graph.

After filling in all 30 NHL teams, here's what the scatter plot looks like for the 2010–2011 regular season. For the most part, the point totals (x axis) tend to rise as the goal totals (y axis) increase. Follow the pattern with a diagonal line and

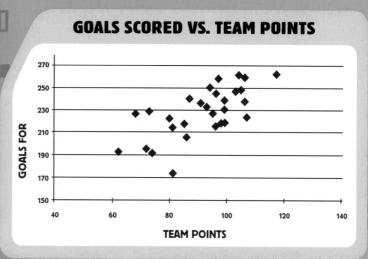

GOALS SCORED VS. TEAM POINTS

keep an equal number of plots above and below the line. You should see a positive correlation. The line—called the line of best fit—can also be used to predict results. For instance, five teams had 87 to 89 points that season, and their goal totals ranged from 217 to 238 points. The line of best fit puts an 88-point season right around 230 goals.

Since defense is just as important as offense, let's compare points with goals allowed. Is there a correlation?

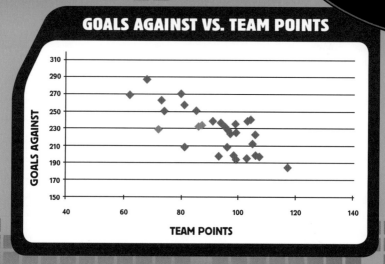

GOALS AGAINST VS. TEAM POINTS

Yes, the line of best fit shows a correlation. For the most part, teams that allow fewer goals have more success in the win column. The team that allowed the most goals—the Colorado Avalanche with 287—ranked second-to-last in total points (68).

CHARTING THE TRENDS

Charts and graphs are a great way to paint a picture of what the numbers are telling you. They are also used to compare changes, trends, and the relationships between statistics.

You can use a line graph to see trends in goal scoring. Are the top NHL players scoring more goals today than 10 years ago? Twenty years ago? Fifty years ago? Is goal scoring going up consistently or going down consistently? Or does it go up and down over time?

To get an idea of the scoring trend, let's look at the league's top scorers over time.

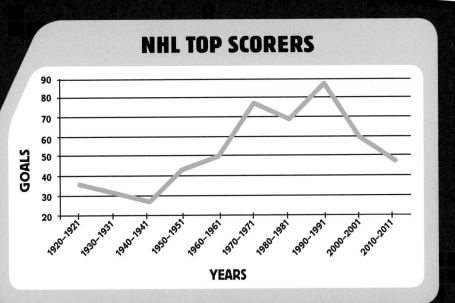

NHL TOP SCORERS

The chart shows an umbrella trend, meaning the numbers start low, rise in the middle, and end low.

Now let's use a bar graph to compare Stanley Cup titles. The Montreal Canadiens have won 24 NHL championships, by far more than any other team. How does their total compare to other current teams that have won the Stanley Cup?

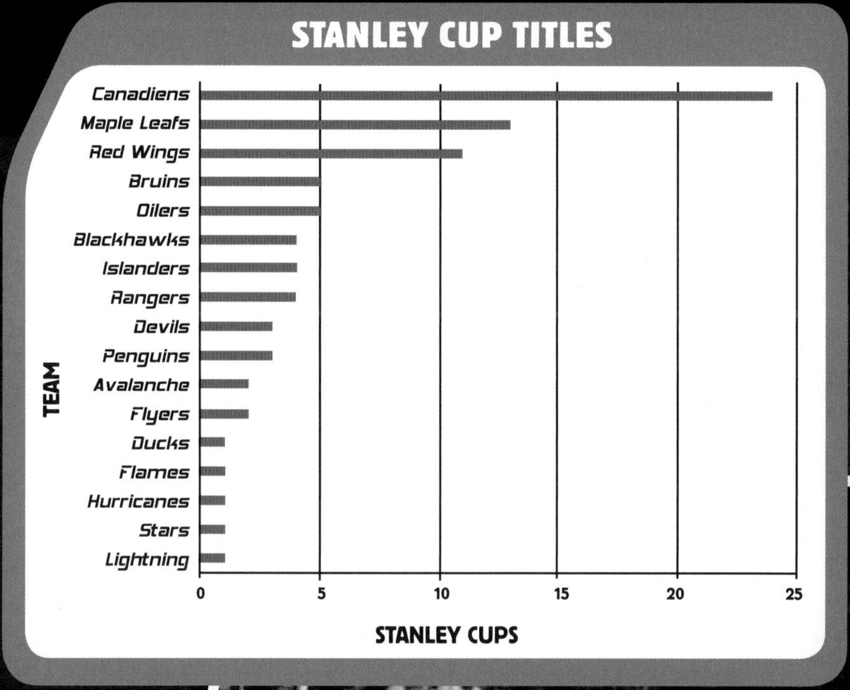
STANLEY CUP TITLES
Canadiens
Maple Leafs
Red Wings
Bruins
Oilers
Blackhawks
Islanders
Rangers
Devils
Penguins
Avalanche
Flyers
Ducks
Flames
Hurricanes
Stars
Lightning
TEAM
0
5
10
15
20
25
STANLEY CUPS

The Canadiens have won almost twice as many titles as the next team, the Toronto Maple Leafs. As you near the end of the chart, you'll see five teams that have each won the Stanley Cup one time.

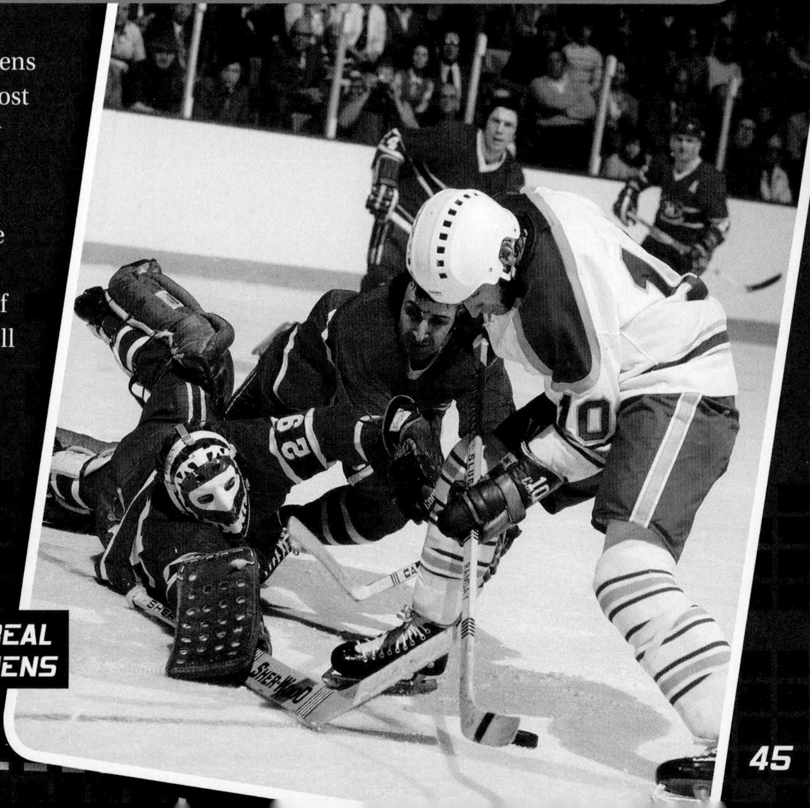

MONTREAL CANADIENS

GLOSSARY

angle of incidence—the incoming line of an angle toward a surface

angle of reflection—the outgoing line of an angle away from a surface

area—the amount of surface within a specific boundary; area is measured in square units

hypotenuse—the longest side of a right triangle

penalty kill—when a shorthanded team denies the other team a goal during a power play

perpendicular—two lines that form a 90-degree angle

plus-minus—a statistic that shows a player's effectiveness; plus-minus is calculated from goals scored and goals allowed while a player is on the ice

power play—when a team has an advantage in the number of players on the ice because of a penalty committed by the other team

Pythagorean theorem—an equation used to find the third side of a right triangle ($a^2 + b^2 = c^2$)

ratio—a comparison of two quantities expressed in numbers

red zone—area inside the attacking zone from which most goals are scored

supplementary angles—two angles that add up to 180 degrees

trapezoid—a four-sided shape with only two parallel sides

READ MORE

Biskup, Agnieszka. *Hockey: How it Works.* The Science of Sports. Mankato, Minn.: Capstone Press, 2010.

Frederick, Shane. *The Best of Everything Hockey Book.* All-Time Best of Sports. Mankato, Minn.: Capstone Press, 2011.

Mahaney, Ian F. *The Math of Hockey.* Sports Math. New York: PowerKids Press, 2011.

INTERNET SITES

FactHound offers a safe, fun way to find Internet sites related to this book. All of the sites on FactHound have been researched by our staff.

Here's all you do:

Visit *www.facthound.com*

Type in this code: 9781429665704

 Check out projects, games and lots more at
www.capstonekids.com

INDEX